Qingming Day

Remembering Family

It is spring.

3

This is my family.

Spring is a special time
for my family.

5

We sweep the leaves

in spring.

We sweep

and we sweep

and we sweep.

Look at the flowers.

We put the flowers here

in spring.

Look at the food.

We put the food here

in spring.

11

Look at this.

We burn this in spring.

Look at the kites.

We will fly kites in spring.

up.

up,

The kites go up, up,

We are with our family

in spring.